Our
Cake Mix
Recipes

Copyright 2012, Gooseberry Patch

First Printing, March, 2012

Substitute pineapple, apple or orange juice for water
in packaged cake mixes for extra flavor.

Pineapple Pig Cake

18-1/2 oz. pkg. yellow cake mix
8-oz. can crushed pineapple,
    drained
11-oz. can mandarin oranges,
    drained and chopped

9-oz. container frozen whipped
    topping, thawed
3.4-oz. pkg. instant vanilla
    pudding mix

Prepare cake mix according to package directions; bake in a greased
13"x9" baking pan. Mix remaining ingredients in a bowl and chill while
cake is baking. Let cake cool; spread pineapple mixture over cake.
Keep refrigerated.

A tier of cake plates is a fun way to serve cookies,
candies and brownies on a buffet table.

Pistachio Cake

Makes 10 to 12 servings

18-1/4 oz. pkg. white cake mix
2 3.4 oz. pkgs. instant pistachio
    pudding mix, divided
3 eggs, beaten
1 c. lemon-lime soda

1 c. oil
1 c. chopped pecans, divided
1-1/2 c. cold milk
2 c. whipped topping

Stir together dry cake mix, one package dry pudding mix, eggs, lemon-lime soda, oil and 1/2 cup pecans; beat at medium speed for 4 minutes. Pour batter into a greased and floured 13"x9" baking dish. Bake at 350 degrees for 40 minutes or until cake tests done; cool. Blend together remaining dry pudding mix and cold milk; beat for 2 minutes. Fold in whipped topping and spread on cake. Sprinkle with remaining pecans; refrigerate one to 2 hours before serving.

When frosting a layer cake, tuck strips of wax paper
under the edges of the bottom layer. Remove them
after the cake is frosted for a neat and tidy cake plate
with no frosting smudges.

Best Chocolate Cake Ever

Serves 16

3.4-oz. pkg. cook & serve
   chocolate pudding mix
2 c. milk
18-1/4 oz. pkg. chocolate cake
   mix

12-oz. pkg. semi-sweet or milk
   chocolate chips
1 c. pecan halves

Lightly grease a 13"x9" baking pan with non-stick vegetable spray.
Prepare chocolate pudding mix with milk according to package directions.
Pour dry cake mix into a bowl; slowly add pudding, stirring constantly
to prevent clumping. Batter will be sticky. Spread into prepared pan.
Sprinkle with chocolate chips and pecans. Bake at 350 degrees for
45 to 48 minutes, or until a toothpick inserted into the center of the
cake comes out clean. Cool before serving.

Create a festive centerpiece in a jiffy! Arrange colorful
fruit on a tier of cake stands. Set a vase of several
blossoms in the center.

Italian Love Cake

Serves 12

18-1/4 oz. pkg. marble cake mix
32-oz. container ricotta cheese
4 eggs, beaten
3/4 c. sugar
1 T. vanilla extract

1 c. milk
3.4-oz. pkg. instant vanilla
   pudding mix
8-oz. container frozen whipped
   topping, thawed

Prepare cake mix according to package directions. Pour batter into a greased and floured 13"x9" baking pan; set aside. In a large bowl, mix together ricotta cheese, eggs, sugar and vanilla. Carefully pour mixture over cake batter; do not stir. Bake at 350 degrees for 70 minutes. Cool cake completely in pan. In a bowl, whisk together milk and dry pudding mix; fold in whipped topping. Spread over cooled cake. Refrigerate until serving time.

A soda shoppe treat...enjoy a pink or brown cow! Just place
a heaping scoop of vanilla ice cream in a thick glass mug,
then add some red pop or root beer and enjoy.

Root Beer Cake

18-1/4 oz. pkg. white cake mix
1-3/4 to 2-1/4 c. chilled root beer,
    divided

1/4 c. oil
2 eggs, beaten
1 env. whipped topping mix

Beat dry cake mix, 1-1/4 cups root beer, oil and eggs together; spread into a greased 13"x9" baking pan. Bake at 350 degrees for 30 to 35 minutes; cool completely. In a chilled bowl, with an electric mixer on medium speed, beat 1/2 cup root beer with whipped topping mix until soft peaks form, adding more root beer if needed. Frost cake. Keep refrigerated.

Life is uncertain. Eat dessert first.

—Ernestine Ulmer

Holy Cow Cake

Makes 16 to 20 servings

18-1/2 oz. pkg. German chocolate
  cake mix
14-oz. can sweetened condensed
  milk
12-1/4 oz. jar caramel ice cream
  topping
2.1-oz. chocolate-covered crispy
  peanut butter candy bar,
  crushed and divided

8-oz. container frozen whipped
  topping, thawed
8-oz. pkg. cream cheese, softened
1 c. sugar

Prepare cake mix according to package directions; bake in a greased
13"x9" baking pan. While cake is baking, stir together condensed milk
and caramel topping; set aside. Remove cake from oven. While cake is
still hot, poke holes in top with a wooden spoon handle or skewer. Pour
condensed milk mixture over cake; sprinkle with half of crushed candy
bar. Refrigerate 2 to 3 hours. Mix together remaining ingredients until
smooth; spread over chilled cake. Sprinkle with remaining candy bar.
Keep refrigerated.

An old-fashioned cake walk is still fun today! Played like musical chairs, each person stands in front of a number placed on the floor. When the music stops, a number is called out and whoever is standing nearest that number gets to take their pick of the baked goodies.

Slice of Sunshine Cake

Serves 12 to 15

18-1/2 oz. pkg. lemon cake mix
3-oz. pkg. orange gelatin mix
1 c. boiling water

1/2 c. orange juice
8-oz. container frozen whipped
    topping, thawed

Prepare cake mix according to package directions; bake in a greased 13"x9" baking pan. Cool. Poke holes over the top of the cake with a fork or skewer. Dissolve gelatin mix in water; stir in orange juice. Pour over cake; cover and refrigerate overnight. Frost with whipped topping before serving.

Pressed-glass jars can store everything from flour and
sugar to cookie cutters and tins of sprinkles! Easily found
at tag sales or flea markets, they'll bring back
fond memories of Mom's kitchen.

Hornet's Nest Cake

4.6-oz. pkg. cook & serve vanilla
   pudding mix
18-1/2 oz. pkg. yellow cake mix

2 c. butterscotch chips
1 c. chopped walnuts

Prepare pudding mix as directed on package; cool to room temperature.
Stir dry cake mix into prepared pudding; blend well. Pour into a greased
13"x9" baking pan; sprinkle with butterscotch chips and walnuts. Bake
at 350 degrees for 35 to 40 minutes, until a toothpick inserted in center
of cake comes out clean.

Scoop portions of Piña Colada Cake into stemmed glasses and top with a dollop of whipped cream and a paper umbrella...fun!

Piña Colada Cake

Makes 8 to 10 servings

18-1/2 oz. pkg. yellow cake mix
15-oz. can cream of coconut
8-oz. can crushed pineapple,
    drained

2 c. frozen whipped topping,
    thawed
2 T. sweetened flaked coconut,
    toasted

Prepare cake mix according to package directions; bake in a greased 13"x9" baking pan. When cake has cooled, use a fork to poke holes in the top. Spread cream of coconut evenly over top of cake. Sprinkle with pineapple; spread whipped topping over entire surface. Sprinkle with coconut. Keep refrigerated.

Put "eat chocolate" at the top of your list of things to do today.
That way, at least you'll get one thing done.

—Unknown

Slow-Cooker Triple Chocolate Cake
Serves 8 to 10

18-1/2 oz. pkg. chocolate cake
    mix
8-oz. container sour cream
3.9-oz. pkg. instant chocolate
    pudding mix
12-oz. pkg. semi-sweet chocolate
    chips

4 eggs, beaten
3/4 c. oil
1 c. water
Garnish: vanilla ice cream

Place all ingredients except ice cream in a slow cooker; mix well. Cover and cook on high setting for 3 to 4 hours. Serve warm, garnished with scoops of ice cream.

Make your own colored sugar...it's simple! Shake together
1/2 cup sugar and 5 to 7 drops food coloring in a
small jar. Spread sugar on a baking sheet to dry.

Rainbow Cake

16-oz. pkg. angel food cake mix
red, blue, yellow and green food
    coloring

Garnish: powdered sugar

Prepare cake mix following package directions; do not pour into tube pan. Place one cup batter into each of 4 different bowls; tint one pink, one blue, one yellow and one green. Spread pink batter into a greased and floured tube pan; carefully spoon blue batter on top. Repeat with yellow and then green batters. Carefully place on lowest rack of oven, bake according to package directions. Remove from oven; invert onto a serving platter. Let cool; sprinkle with powdered sugar.

For blue-ribbon perfect chocolate cakes with no white
streaks, use baking cocoa instead of flour
to dust greased pans.

Chocolate Spice Cake

Serves 12

18-1/4 oz. pkg. German chocolate
   cake mix
1-1/2 t. cinnamon

3 eggs, beaten
12-oz. can date pie filling

Combine dry cake mix and cinnamon; add eggs and pie filling, stirring until just moistened. Spread in a greased tube pan. Bake at 350 degrees for 55 minutes to one hour. Cool; remove from pan.

Use a long strand of spaghetti to test
the doneness of deep cakes.

Rum Cake

18-1/4 oz. pkg. golden butter
    cake mix
4 eggs, beaten

1/2 c. oil
1/2 c. water
1/2 c. light rum

In a bowl with an electric mixer on medium speed, beat all ingredients together for 2 minutes. Pour into a greased and floured Bundt® pan. Bake at 325 degrees for 50 to 60 minutes. Remove cake from pan immediately; pour Rum Sauce over warm cake.

Rum Sauce:

1 c. sugar
1/2 c. butter

1/4 c. water
1/4 c. light rum

In a small saucepan, cook ingredients together for 3 to 5 minutes.

For a decorative finish on a frosted cake,
create wavy lines by drawing the tines of
a fork through the frosting.

Cookies & Cream Cake

18-1/4 oz. pkg. white cake mix
1-1/4 c. water
1/3 c. oil

3 egg whites
1 c. chocolate sandwich cookies,
    crushed

Combine dry cake mix, water, oil and egg whites in a large bowl; blend until just moistened. Beat on high speed with an electric mixer for 2 minutes; gently fold in crushed cookies. Divide and pour equally into 2 greased and floured 8" round cake pans. Bake at 350 degrees for 30 minutes, or until a toothpick inserted in the center removes clean. Cool for 10 minutes; remove from pans to a wire rack to cool completely. Frost.

Frosting:
4 to 4-1/2 c. powdered sugar
1/2 c. shortening

1/4 c. milk
1 t. vanilla extract

Blend all ingredients together until smooth and creamy.

Dress up a plain cake...lay a paper doily on top, then sprinkle with powdered sugar or baking cocoa. So dainty, yet so simple!

Comforting Southern Cake

Serves 10 to 12

18-1/2 oz. pkg. yellow cake mix
3.4-oz. pkg. instant vanilla
    pudding mix
4 eggs, beaten
1/2 c. cold water
1/2 c. oil
1/2 c. peach-flavored bourbon or
    orange juice
1-1/2 c. chopped nuts
Garnish: powdered sugar

Combine all ingredients except nuts and powdered sugar; beat with an electric mixer on medium speed for 3 minutes. Stir in nuts; pour into a greased and floured Bundt® pan. Bake at 325 degrees for one hour. While cake is still hot, pierce all over with a skewer; slowly pour Glaze over top. Cool in pan. Invert onto a plate; sprinkle with sugar.

Glaze:

1/4 c. butter
2 T. water
1/2 c. sugar
1/4 c. peach-flavored bourbon or
    orange juice

Melt butter in a saucepan over medium heat. Stir in water and sugar; boil for 3 minutes, stirring constantly. Remove from heat; stir in bourbon or orange juice.

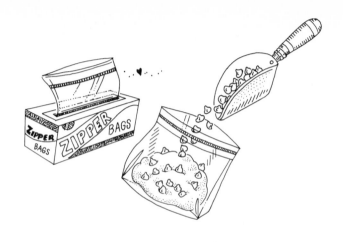

A time-saving tip! Fill plastic zipping bags with dry
ingredients for favorite baked recipes... just add
the wet ingredients later.

Hootenanny Cake

Makes 8 to 10 servings

18-1/4 oz. pkg. yellow cake mix
3.4-oz. pkg. instant coconut
    pudding mix
1/2 t. baking powder
1 c. water
4 eggs, beaten

1/2 c. oil
1 t. vanilla extract
1 c. chopped pecans
4 t. sugar
2 t. cinnamon

Mix together dry cake mix, dry pudding mix, baking powder, water, eggs, oil and vanilla; set aside. Blend together pecans, sugar and cinnamon. Spread one-third of pecan mixture in a lightly greased tube pan. Top with half the cake batter. Sprinkle another one-third of pecan mixture on top of cake batter, then pour remaining cake batter into pan. Top with remaining pecan mixture. Bake at 350 degrees for 50 minutes to one hour, until cake tests done with a long skewer.

To freeze fresh berries, arrange them in a single layer
on a baking sheet and place in your freezer. Once frozen,
transfer to freezer bags.

Mom's Blackberry Cake

Serves 10 to 12

18-1/2 oz. pkg. white cake mix
    with pudding
3-oz. pkg. red raspberry gelatin
    mix
1 c. oil

1/2 c. milk
4 eggs
1 c. blackberries
1 c. sweetened flaked coconut
1 c. chopped pecans

Combine dry cake and pudding mixes with oil and milk; mix well. Add eggs, one at a time, beating well after each addition. Fold in blackberries, coconut and pecans. Pour into 3 greased 9" round cake pans. Bake at 350 degrees for 25 to 30 minutes. Cool for 10 minutes before removing to wire racks to cool completely. Spread tops of layers with frosting and assemble cake. Spread remaining frosting over sides.

Frosting:

1/2 c. butter, softened
16-oz. pkg. powdered sugar
4 to 5 T. milk

1/2 c. blackberries, crushed
1/2 c. sweetened flaked coconut
1/2 c. chopped pecans

Beat together butter and powdered sugar. Add milk and berries; beat for 2 minutes. Stir in coconut and pecans.

Look for vintage pie plates, servers and cake stands at flea markets...add them to your own collection or make them part of the gift when sharing a favorite sweet treat.

Butter Pecan Cake

Makes 10 to 12 servings

18-oz. pkg. butter pecan cake mix
15-oz. can coconut-pecan frosting
3 eggs, beaten
3/4 c. oil
1 c. water
1/2 c. chopped pecans
Garnish: vanilla ice cream

In a large bowl, combine dry cake mix with remaining ingredients except ice cream. Stir to blend; beat for 2 minutes with an electric mixer on high speed. Pour into a greased and floured Bundt® pan. Bake at 350 degrees for 55 minutes, or until cake tests done with a skewer. Cool for 15 minutes before inverting onto a serving plate. Serve slices topped with scoops of ice cream.

To make a cake extra rich, substitute two egg yolks
for each whole egg.

Boston Cream Cake

Servings 12

18-1/2 oz. pkg. yellow cake mix
5-1/4 oz. pkg. instant vanilla
    pudding mix

16-oz. container chocolate
    frosting
Garnish: 1 maraschino cherry

Prepare cake mix according to package directions, using two 9" round cake pans. Cool; remove from pans. Prepare pudding mix according to package directions; refrigerate. Spread pudding over one cake layer, but stay about one inch away from the edges. Place second cake layer on top. Microwave frosting on high at 20 second intervals, stirring between, until frosting is pourable but not boiling (the consistency of thick syrup). Let cool a few minutes; spoon over the top of the cake until the top is covered and it runs down the sides. Put a maraschino cherry in the center. Refrigerate until serving time.

Need to peel peaches or pears in a hurry? Simply scald them
in hot water, then submerge them in cold water...
the skins will peel right off.

Quick Peach Crumble

15-oz. can diced peaches   2 t. cinnamon
18-1/2 oz. pkg. yellow cake mix   1/4 c. butter, melted

Pour peaches and their juice into a greased 13"x9" baking pan. Sprinkle dry cake mix and cinnamon on top. Drizzle melted butter over all. Bake at 375 degrees for 35 to 40 minutes, until golden on top and bubbly on the sides.

Before cutting a cake into cubes for a trifle, freeze and
then partially thaw it. There will be fewer crumbs
and more cake to enjoy!

All-American Trifle

Serves 15

18-1/2 oz. pkg. white cake mix
1 qt. strawberries, hulled, sliced
   in half and divided
1 pt. blueberries, divided
1 pt. raspberries, divided

1 pt. blackberries, divided
raspberry liqueur or ice cream
   syrup
16-oz. container frozen whipped
   topping, thawed and divided

Prepare cake according to package directions; pour batter into a greased 9"x9" baking pan. Bake as directed; cool. Cut cake into one-inch cubes. Arrange one layer of cake cubes in a trifle bowl; scatter a layer of strawberry slices between the cake squares. Top with a layer of blueberries, raspberries and blackberries; drizzle raspberry liqueur or syrup over the top. Spread with a thin layer of whipped topping; repeat layers until no more cake remains. Chill until ready to serve.

Create a pretty marbleized effect when baking a white
cake mix. After the batter has been poured into a cake pan,
simply sprinkle with a few drops of food coloring, then swirl
the color around with a knife tip.

Lemonade-Ice Cream Cake

Makes 10 servings

2 pts. vanilla ice cream, softened
7 drops yellow food coloring
6-oz. can frozen lemonade
    concentrate, thawed and
    divided

18-1/2 oz. pkg. yellow cake mix
2 c. whipping cream
2-1/2 T. sugar

Combine ice cream, food coloring and 1/2 cup lemonade concentrate; spread evenly in an aluminum foil-lined, 9" round baking pan. Freeze until firm, about 2 to 3 hours. Prepare and bake cake mix following package instructions for two 9" round cakes; cool. Place one cake layer on a serving plate; top with frozen ice cream layer and remaining cake layer. Freeze. In a chilled bowl, with an electric mixer on high speed, beat whipping cream with remaining lemonade and sugar until fluffy and peaks form; frost cake. Freeze at least one more hour before serving.

Decorate baked goods with a sparkling array of sugared
berries...it's easy! Brush berries with light corn syrup,
then sprinkle generously with sanding sugar and allow to dry.

Apple Gingerbread Cobbler

14-oz. pkg. gingerbread cake
   mix, divided
3/4 c. water
1/4 c. brown sugar, packed

1/2 c. butter, divided
1/2 c. chopped pecans
2 21-oz. cans apple pie filling
Garnish: vanilla ice cream

Mix together 2 cups dry gingerbread cake mix and water until smooth;
set aside. In a separate bowl, combine brown sugar and remaining cake
mix; cut in 1/4 cup butter until mixture is crumbly. Stir in pecans; set
aside. Combine pie filling and remaining butter in a large saucepan. Cook,
stirring often, for 5 minutes over medium heat, or until heated through.
Spoon pie filling mixture evenly into a lightly greased 11"x7" baking pan.
Spoon gingerbread batter over apple mixture; sprinkle with brown sugar
mixture. Bake at 375 degrees for 30 to 35 minutes, until set. Serve with
scoops of ice cream.

Decorating dessert plates is so easy and fun. Try drizzling
fruity syrups along the edges or pipe on melted chocolate
in fun designs and words.

Coconut Freezer Cake

Makes 12 to 18 servings

18-1/4 oz. pkg. white cake mix
14-oz. pkg. sweetened flaked
    coconut
16-oz. container sour cream

2 c. sugar
8-oz. container frozen whipped
    topping, thawed

Prepare cake mix according to package directions, dividing batter evenly among 3 greased 9" round cake pans. Bake according to package directions. Let cool. In a large bowl, combine coconut, sour cream and sugar; set aside one cup of mixture. Place one cake layer on a cake stand and top with half the coconut mixture. Add second cake layer and spread remaining coconut mixture on top. Top with third layer; set aside. Combine reserved coconut mixture with whipped topping; frost top and sides of cake. Place in freezer. Let stand 15 minutes before serving.

Upside-down pineapple cupcakes are an unexpected treat. Place a tablespoon of crushed pineapple into each greased muffin cup and top with a teaspoonful of brown sugar and melted butter. Fill cups halfway with yellow cake mix batter and bake according to package directions. Turn out of cups to serve.

Cherry Crisp Cobbler

Makes 8 servings

14-1/2 oz. can cherry pie filling
18-1/2 oz. pkg. white cake mix
2 T. brown sugar, packed
1 t. cinnamon

1/2 c. chopped pecans
1/2 c. margarine, melted
Optional: vanilla ice cream

Spread pie filling in a lightly greased 8"x8" glass baking pan; set aside.
Combine dry cake mix, brown sugar, cinnamon and pecans; mix well
and sprinkle over pie filling. Drizzle with magarine; microwave on high
for 13 minutes. Let stand for 5 minutes; cut into squares. Serve topped
with ice cream, if desired.

Leftover canned pumpkin? Try stirring it into softened
vanilla ice cream for a frosty treat.

Crustless Pumpkin Pie

Makes 8 to 10 servings

4 eggs, beaten
15-oz. can pumpkin
12-oz. can evaporated milk
1-1/2 c. sugar
2 t. pumpkin pie spice
1 t. salt

18-1/2 oz. pkg. yellow cake mix
1 c. chopped pecans
1 c. butter, melted
Garnish: whipped topping,
  chopped walnuts, cinnamon
  or nutmeg

Combine eggs, pumpkin, evaporated milk, sugar, spice and salt. Mix well and pour into an ungreased 13"x9" baking pan. Sprinkle dry cake mix and nuts over top. Drizzle with butter; do not stir. Bake at 350 degrees for 45 minutes to one hour, testing for doneness with a toothpick. Serve with whipped topping sprinkled with nuts and cinnamon or nutmeg.

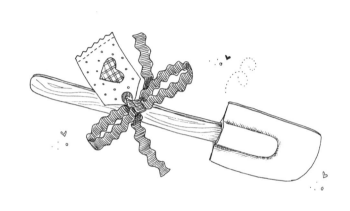

An 18-1/2 oz. packaged cake mix will make two 8- or 9-inch
round layers, one 13x9-inch sheet cake or 24 cupcakes.

Upside-Down German Chocolate Cake

Makes 15 to 18 servings

18-1/4 oz. pkg. German chocolate cake mix
4-oz. pkg. sweetened flaked coconut
4-oz. pkg. chopped walnuts
8-oz. pkg. cream cheese, softened
1/2 c. butter, softened
2 c. powdered sugar

Prepare cake mix as directed on the package. Sprinkle coconut in a greased and floured 13"x9" baking pan; sprinkle walnuts on top. Pour cake batter over coconut and walnuts. In a bowl, combine cream cheese, butter and powdered sugar; blend to a smooth consistency. Take large spoonfuls of mixture and dot over cake batter. Swirl together cake batter and cream cheese mixture with a table knife. Bake as directed on cake mix package for a 13"x9" pan.

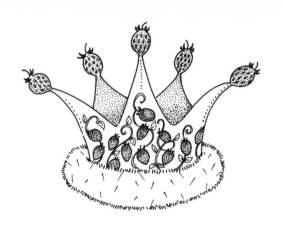

Top cakes with a strawberry fan...starting at the tip,
cut a strawberry into thin slices almost to the stem.
Carefully spread slices to form a fan.

The Queen's Strawberry Cake

10-oz. pkg. frozen strawberries,
    thawed
18-1/4 oz. pkg. white cake mix
1/2 c. water

1/2 c. oil
4 eggs
3-oz. pkg. strawberry gelatin mix

Drain strawberries; reserve 1/3 cup juice and set aside. Combine dry cake mix, water and oil in a bowl; beat until smooth. Add eggs, one at a time, beating after each addition. Add half of the strawberries and reserved juice. Add dry gelatin mix; blend well. Pour into a greased 13"x9" pan; spoon remaining strawberries on top. Bake at 350 degrees for 30 to 40 minutes. Let cool; invert onto a serving plate.

To make it a little easier to transfer filled cake cones
to the oven, stand cones in a 13x9-inch baking pan or
in the cups of a muffin tin.

Celebration Cake Cones

18-1/2 oz. pkg. favorite cake mix
1/2 c. plus 3 T. water
2 eggs, beaten
1 t. vanilla extract

1 T. oil
24 flat-bottomed ice cream cones
Garnish: frosting, candy sprinkles

Combine dry cake mix and 1/2 cup water; beat for one minute. Add eggs, remaining water, vanilla and oil; mix well. Wrap aluminum foil around bottoms of cones; place in muffin cups. Fill each cone 1/2 full with batter. Bake at 400 degrees for 15 minutes, or until cake springs back when touched. Cool completely; decorate as desired.

Oh-so cute! Insert a wooden craft stick in each
Taffy Apple Cupcake and arrange them on a tray
for a festive presentation.

Taffy Apple Cupcakes

Makes one dozen

18-1/4 oz. pkg. carrot cake mix
1 c. Granny Smith apples, peeled,
    cored and finely chopped
1/2 t. cinnamon
20 caramels, unwrapped

1/4 c. milk
1 c. pecans or walnuts, finely
    chopped
12 wooden craft sticks

Prepare cake mix according to package instructions; stir in apples
and cinnamon. Fill paper-lined jumbo muffin cups 2/3 full. Bake at
350 degrees for 20 to 25 minutes, until a toothpick inserted near center
tests clean. Combine caramels and milk in a small saucepan over low
heat; stir until melted and smooth. Spread caramel over cooled cupcakes;
sprinkle nuts over top. Insert a craft stick into center of each cupcake.

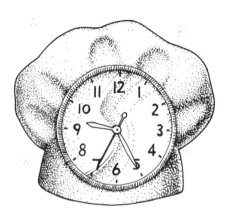

No peeking! When baking, the temperature drops
25 degrees every time the oven door is opened.

Strawberry Angel Food Roll

Serves 10 to 12

14-1/2 oz. pkg. angel food cake
    mix
1 qt. strawberries, hulled and
    sliced

1/4 c. sugar
2 c. whipping cream
3 T. powdered sugar

Prepare cake mix according to package directions; pour into a greased
15"x10" jelly-roll pan lined with wax paper. Bake at 375 degrees for 10
to 12 minutes. Turn cake onto a tea towel dusted with powdered sugar.
Peel off wax paper. Starting at narrow end, roll up cake and towel
together; cool on wire rack for 20 minutes, seam-side down. In a bowl,
combine strawberries and sugar; set aside. In a separate bowl, beat cream
with an electric mixer on medium speed until foamy. Add powdered
sugar; continue beating until soft peaks form. Drain any liquid from
berries. Unroll cake; set towel aside. Spread cake with half the whipped
cream mixture; top with strawberries. Re-roll cake; place on a plate
seam-side down. Slice to serve; top with remaining whipped cream.

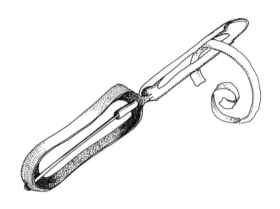

Chocolate curls are so elegant! Soften a bar of white or milk chocolate by microwaving for 8 seconds at a time, until softened. Use a sharp vegetable peeler and peel toward you to make curls.

Choco-Mallow Cake

12-oz. pkg. marshmallows, divided

18-1/4 oz. pkg. yellow cake mix
12-oz. pkg. dark chocolate chips

Place half the marshmallows in a 13"x9" baking pan that has been sprayed with non-stick vegetable spray; set aside. Reserve remaining marshmallows for another recipe. Prepare cake mix according to package directions. Pour batter over marshmallows in the pan. Sprinkle chocolate chips over top. Bake at 350 degrees for 32 to 37 minutes. Marshmallows will rise to top of cake and chocolate chips will sink to bottom.

Do you have extra coffee? Pour it into an ice cube tray and freeze. It will be easy to add just a hint of mocha to all your favorite chocolate recipes!

Red Velvet Cake

Makes 10 to 12 servings

18-1/4 oz. pkg. fudge marble
    cake mix
1 t. baking soda
2 eggs, beaten

1-1/2 c. buttermilk
1-oz. bottle red food coloring
1 t. vanilla extract
16-oz. container vanilla frosting

Combine dry cake mix and baking soda in a medium bowl; add
remaining ingredients. Blend with an electric mixer on low speed until
moistened. Beat on high speed for 2 minutes. Pour batter into 2 greased
and floured 9" round cake pans. Bake at 350 degrees for 30 to
35 minutes, until cake tests done. Cool in pans for 10 minutes; turn out
onto a wire rack. Cool completely; if desired, freeze layers overnight to
make cake easier to frost. Frost between layers, top and sides of cake. If
frozen, thaw one hour before serving.

For special guests, serve up individual servings of trifle
in parfait glasses or Mason jars.

Pumpkin Trifle

14-1/2 oz. pkg. gingerbread
  cake mix
1-1/4 c. water
1 egg, beaten
4 c. milk
4 1-oz. pkgs. sugar-free instant
  butterscotch pudding mix

15-oz. can pumpkin
1 t. cinnamon
1/4 t. ground ginger
1/4 t. nutmeg
1/4 t. allspice
12-oz. container frozen whipped
  topping, thawed

Combine dry cake mix, water and egg in a bowl. Mix well; pour into an ungreased 8"x8" baking pan. Bake at 350 degrees for 35 to 40 minutes, until a toothpick inserted near the center comes out clean. Cool for 10 minutes; turn out of pan onto a wire rack. When completely cooled; crumble cake and set aside, reserving 1/4 cup crumbs for garnish. Whisk together milk and pudding mixes in a bowl for 2 minutes, or until slightly thickened. Let stand for 2 minutes, or until softly set. Stir in pumpkin and spices; mix well. In a trifle bowl, layer one-quarter of cake crumbs, half of pudding mixture, one-quarter of crumbs and one-half of whipped topping. Repeat layers, ending with topping. Garnish with reserved cake crumbs. Serve immediately or refrigerate.

For an extra-special touch, roll cake balls in colored or
cinnamon-sugar, chopped nuts, flaked coconut
or colored sprinkles.

Cake Balls

Makes 4 dozen

18-1/4 oz. favorite-flavor cake mix
16-oz. container favorite-flavor frosting, divided

20-oz. pkg. dark or white melting chocolate, chopped

Prepare cake mix according to package directions; bake in a 13"x 9" baking pan. Let cake cool. Turn cake into a large bowl and crumble into small pieces. Add half of frosting; reserve the other half for another use. Mix well. Roll mixture into one-inch balls; refrigerate for about an hour. Place chocolate in a microwave-safe container. Microwave on high for 60 seconds. Stir; continue cooking on high for another 30 seconds, or until completely melted. Stir until smooth. Dip balls into melted chocolate with a fork or a candy dipping tool; place on wax paper-lined baking sheets. Place in refrigerator again for about 10 minutes, until chocolate sets. Store in an airtight container.

A melon baller is a great tool for
making uniformly sized cookies.

Chocolate Whoopie Pies

Makes 4 dozen

2 18-1/4 oz. pkgs. devil's food cake mix
4 eggs, beaten
2/3 c. oil

Beat together dry cake mixes, eggs and oil; dough will be very stiff. Roll into one-inch balls; arrange on ungreased baking sheets. Flatten balls slightly; bake at 350 degrees for 8 to 10 minutes. Cool on baking sheets for 3 minutes; remove to wire rack. Spread Frosting on the bottom of a cookie; place another cookie on top. Repeat with remaining cookies and frosting.

Frosting:
1 c. milk
5 T. all-purpose flour
1/2 c. butter, softened
1/2 c. shortening
1 c. sugar
1 t. vanilla extract

Combine milk and flour in a saucepan over medium heat; cook and stir until thickened. Cover and refrigerate until chilled. In a separate bowl, beat together butter, shortening, sugar and vanilla until creamy. Add chilled milk mixture; beat for 10 minutes with an electric mixer on medium speed.

Parchment paper is a baker's best friend! Place it on a baking sheet to keep cookies from spreading and sticking...clean-up is a breeze too.

Raisin Spice Cookies

Makes 1-1/2 dozen

18-1/2 oz. pkg. spice cake mix   1/3 c. oil
2 eggs   3/4 c. raisins

Mix dry cake mix and remaining ingredients together; drop by rounded
teaspoonfuls onto ungreased baking sheets. Bake at 350 degrees for
12 to 15 minutes. Let cool for 5 minutes before removing from
baking sheets.

Tea towels can be found in such pretty patterns and colors.
For a welcome surprise, fill a plate with cookies, then wrap
the plate in a new tea towel to match the colors
in a friend's kitchen.

Pecan Pie Bars

Makes about 2 dozen

18-1/2 oz. pkg. yellow cake mix, divided
1/2 c. butter, melted
1 egg, beaten
1/2 c. brown sugar, packed
1-1/2 c. light corn syrup
3 eggs, beaten
1 t. vanilla extract
1 c. chopped pecans

Set aside 2/3 cup dry cake mix for filling. In a large bowl, combine remaining cake mix, butter and egg; mix well. Press into a greased 13"x9" baking pan. Bake at 350 degrees for 15 to 20 minutes, until lightly golden; remove and set aside. In a large bowl, combine reserved cake mix, brown sugar, corn syrup, eggs and vanilla. Beat for 2 minutes with an electric mixer on medium speed. Stir in pecans and pour over baked crust. Bake at 350 degrees for an additional 30 to 35 minutes, until almost set. Cool; slice into bars.

Crushed toffee or peppermint candy makes a festive topping
for rich brownies. Simply place candy in a plastic zipping bag and
tap gently with a kitchen mallet until candy is broken up.

Millionaire Brownies

Makes 2 dozen

18-1/4 oz. pkg. chocolate fudge
    cake mix
1 c. evaporated milk, divided
3/4 c. butter, softened

14-oz. pkg. caramels, unwrapped
1-1/2 c. semi-sweet chocolate
    chips
1-1/2 c. chopped pecans

Stir dry cake mix, 2/3 cup evaporated milk and butter until moistened. Spread half the mixture in a greased 13"x9" baking pan. Bake at 350 degrees for 8 minutes; cool. Combine caramels and remaining evaporated milk in a small saucepan over low heat, stir constantly, until caramels are melted. Sprinkle brownies with chocolate chips; drizzle with caramel mixture. Top with pecans. Spread remaining batter over top. Bake at 350 degrees for 18 to 20 minutes. Cool completely before cutting.

Easy-squeezy! Place frosting ingredients in a
plastic zipping bag. Squeeze to mix well, then snip off
a small corner and squeeze to drizzle over
baked goods...so simple!

Lime Macaroons

Makes about 6 dozen

2 c. lime sherbet
18-1/2 oz. pkg. white cake mix
1-1/2 T. almond extract

2 7-oz. pkgs. sweetened flaked
  coconut

Soften sherbet in a large bowl. Add dry cake mix and extract; blend just until well mixed. Stir in coconut. Drop by rounded teaspoonfuls onto greased baking sheets. Bake at 350 degrees for 10 to 13 minutes, until light golden.

Take a basket of bar cookies to work and place one
on each co-worker's desk with a package of instant
cappuccino...a terrific Monday morning pick-me-up!

Schoolhouse Cookie Bars

Makes 18 to 20 servings

18-1/2 oz. pkg. yellow cake mix
2 c. quick-cooking oats, uncooked
3/4 c. oil
1 egg, beaten

12-oz. jar caramel ice cream
   topping
1 c. semi-sweet chocolate chips
Optional: 1/2 c. chopped nuts

Combine dry cake mix, oats, oil and egg; spread half of batter in a greased 13"x9" baking pan. Drizzle with caramel topping; sprinkle with chocolate chips and nuts. Crumble remaining cake batter over the top; bake at 350 degrees for 28 to 30 minutes. Cut into squares.

When you give goodies in clever containers, they become
part of the gift! Antique fluted pudding molds, old-fashioned
teacups and teapots, hatboxes or vintage cookie jars
are just right for gift-giving. Add your treat inside then
wrap with holiday ribbon or lengths of rick rack.

Mochaccino Chip Cookies

Makes 2 dozen

18-1/2 oz. pkg. devil's food cake
    mix
2 eggs, beaten
1/2 c. oil

2 T. instant cappuccino mix
1 t. vanilla extract
1 c. white chocolate chips

Combine dry cake mix, eggs, oil, cappuccino mix and vanilla in a large
bowl; mix well. Fold in chocolate chips. Drop by teaspoonfuls onto
ungreased baking sheets. Bake at 350 degrees for 10 to 12 minutes.
Allow to cool partially on baking sheets; transfer to a wire rack to
finish cooling.

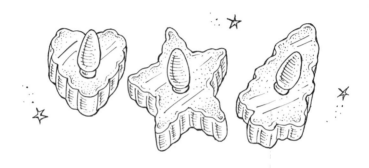

Add a packet of unsweetened powdered drink mix
to a container of vanilla frosting for instantly colored
and flavored frosting!

Cake Mix Cut-Outs

Makes about 3 dozen

18-1/2 oz. pkg. yellow cake mix
1/2 c. butter, softened
1 t. vanilla extract

2 eggs, beaten
Garnish: frosting

In a large bowl, combine all ingredients except frosting; beat until smooth. Roll dough out on a floured surface to 1/4-inch thick; cut into desired shapes with cookie cutters. Place on ungreased baking sheets. Bake at 350 degrees for 12 to 15 minutes, until tops are lightly golden and edges are done. Cool; frost as desired.

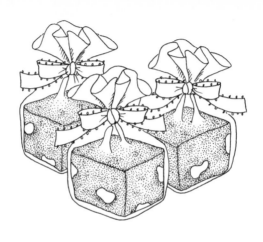

For a change, slice bar cookies into one-inch squares. Guests will love trying "just a bite" of several different treats.

Oatmeal-Raspberry Bars

Makes 15 to 18

18-1/4 oz. pkg. yellow cake mix
3/4 c. butter, melted
2-1/2 c. quick-cooking oats,
    uncooked

12-oz. jar raspberry jam
1 T. warm water

Combine dry cake mix, butter and oats in a large bowl; toss until crumbly. Press half the mixture firmly into a greased 13"x9" baking pan; set aside. Stir jam and water together; spread evenly over crust layer. Cover with remaining crumb mixture, patting firmly; bake at 375 degrees for 20 minutes. Drizzle with Glaze while warm. Cool; slice into bars to serve.

Glaze:
1 c. powdered sugar   2 to 3 T. warm water

Combine powdered sugar with enough water to reach desired drizzling consistency.

FOR YOU!

Fill each cup of an old-fashioned muffin tin with a
different type of cookie...what a tasty sampler!

Lemon Whippersnappers

Makes 4 dozen

18-1/4 oz. pkg. lemon cake mix
2 c. frozen whipped topping,
    thawed

1 egg, beaten
1/2 c. powdered sugar

Combine dry cake mix, whipped topping and egg in a large bowl; stir
until well mixed. Drop by rounded teaspoonfuls into powdered sugar and
roll to coat. Place on greased baking sheets. Bake at 350 degrees for
10 to 15 minutes, until golden. Remove from baking sheet; cool on
wire racks.

Warm cookies dipped in cold milk...one of life's
simple pleasures.

—Unknown

Super-Simple Snickerdoodles

Makes about 2 dozen

18-1/2 oz. pkg. yellow cake mix
2 eggs, beaten
1/2 c. oil

1 T. cinnamon
Garnish: cinnamon-sugar

Combine dry cake mix, eggs, oil and cinnamon in a large bowl; mix well.
Drop by teaspoonfuls onto ungreased baking sheets. Bake at 350 degrees
for 8 to 10 minutes. While still warm, sprinkle with cinnamon-sugar.
Let cool for 2 minutes on baking sheets; transfer to wire racks to
finish cooling.

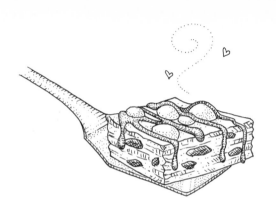

Cookie clean-up is a snap for bar cookies... just line the baking pan with aluminum foil before adding the dough. Once the cookies have completely cooled, lift the cookies out, peel off the foil and cut into bars.

Slow-Poke Turtle Bars

Makes 1-1/2 dozen

18-1/4 oz. pkg. German chocolate
    cake mix
1 c. chopped pecans
3/4 c. margarine, softened

2/3 c. evaporated milk, divided
14-oz. pkg. caramels, unwrapped
6-oz. pkg. semi-sweet chocolate
    chips

In a bowl, combine dry cake mix, pecans, margarine and 1/3 cup evaporated milk. Pat half of the dough into a greased 13"x9" baking pan. Bake at 350 degrees for 6 minutes. In a heavy saucepan, melt caramels and remaining 1/3 cup evaporated milk over low heat. Stir constantly until caramels are completely melted. Sprinkle chocolate chips over dough, then drizzle with caramel mixture. Crumble remaining dough over top. Bake at 350 degrees for 25 minutes. Cut into squares after cooling slightly.

To soften butter quickly for a recipe,
grate chilled sticks with a cheese grater.
The butter will soften in just minutes!

Ladybug Cookies

Makes 3-1/2 dozen

18-1/2 oz. pkg. red velvet cake
    mix
1/2 c. oil

2 eggs, beaten
12-oz. pkg. semi-sweet chocolate
    chips

Combine dry cake mix, oil and eggs; mix well. Stir in chocolate chips;
drop by tablespoonfuls onto ungreased baking sheets. Bake at
350 degrees for 9 to 10 minutes. Cool on wire racks.

Bar cookie dough should always be baked in the pan size
the recipe calls for, to avoid dry or underbaked cookies.

Salted Nut Roll Bars

Makes 2-1/2 dozen

18-1/2 oz. pkg. yellow cake mix
3/4 c. butter, melted and divided
1 egg, beaten
3 c. mini marshmallows
10-oz. pkg. peanut butter chips

1/2 c. light corn syrup
1 t. vanilla extract
2 c. salted peanuts
2 c. crispy rice cereal

In a bowl, combine dry cake mix, 1/4 cup butter and egg; press into a greased 13"x9" baking pan. Bake at 350 degrees for 10 to 12 minutes. Sprinkle marshmallows over baked crust; return to oven and bake for 3 additional minutes, or until marshmallows are melted. In a saucepan over medium heat, melt peanut butter chips, corn syrup, remaining butter and vanilla. Stir in nuts and cereal. Spread mixture over marshmallow layer. Chill briefly until firm; cut into squares.

Sending a care package? Remember some cookies
travel better than others...chocolate chip, snickerdoodles,
oatmeal and brownies don't break easily,
making them ideal for shipping.

Brown Sugar Blondies

Makes 2 dozen

18-1/2 oz. pkg. white cake mix
1/3 c. light brown sugar, packed
2 T. water
1/3 c. oil
2 eggs, beaten

6-oz. pkg. semi-sweet chocolate
  chips
Optional: 1/2 c. chopped walnuts
  or pecans

In a large bowl, combine dry cake mix and remaining ingredients. Mix
well; spread into a greased 13"x9" baking pan. Bake at 350 degrees for
30 minutes. Cool before cutting into squares.

Dip mini cookie cutters into cinnamon or powdered sugar,
then lightly press the image into the frosted tops of
brownies and bars...such a sweet touch!

Dulce de Leche Bars

Makes 10 to 14

18-1/2 oz. pkg. spice cake mix
2 eggs, beaten
1/3 c. unsweetened applesauce
6-oz. pkg. semi-sweet chocolate
    chips

14-oz. can dulce de leche
1/4 c. butter

In a bowl, combine dry cake mix, eggs and applesauce. Stir until
mixture forms a sticky dough. In a 13"x9" baking pan, spread and pat
down 3/4 of mixture; set aside. Combine chocolate chips, dulce de leche
and butter in a microwave-safe bowl. Microwave on high for one to
2 minutes, until melted. Stir well to combine; spread over first layer.
Place large spoonfuls of remaining cake mix mixture on top, flattening
and spreading as much as possible. Bake at 350 degrees for 20 to
25 minutes, until golden. Cool completely before cutting into bars.

For best results when baking, allow butter and eggs
to come to room temperature. Just set them out
on the counter about an hour ahead of time
and they'll be ready!

Rabbit Scones

Makes one dozen

8-oz. pkg. cream cheese, softened
18-1/4 oz. pkg. carrot cake mix
1/3 c. half-and-half
1 egg, beaten
1/2 t. cinnamon

1/4 c. chopped walnuts
1/2 c. raisins
1/2 c. cream cheese frosting,
   warmed

In a large bowl, cut cream cheese into dry cake mix using a fork or a
pastry blender, until mixture resembles fine crumbs. Stir in half-and-half,
egg, cinnamon, walnuts and raisins until soft dough forms. On a floured
surface, knead dough 6 times. Divide dough in half; form each half into a
ball. Press each dough ball into a circle about 6 inches in diameter and
3/4-inch thick. Cut each circle into 6 wedges. Place one inch apart on a
lightly greased baking sheet. Bake at 375 degrees for 18 to 22 minutes,
until edges begin to turn golden. Remove to a wire rack; cool for 10 to
15 minutes. In a small microwave-safe bowl, melt frosting; drizzle
over scones.

Enjoy fresh-baked cookies at a moment's notice. Roll your
favorite cookie dough into balls and freeze on a tray, then pop
them into a freezer bag. Later, just pull out the number of
cookies you need, thaw briefly and bake.

Honey Bun Cake

Serves 12

18-1/2 oz. pkg. yellow cake mix
3/4 c. oil
4 eggs, beaten
8-oz. container sour cream
1 c. brown sugar, packed

1 T. cinnamon
2 c. powdered sugar
1 T. vanilla extract
1/4 c. milk

Stir dry cake mix, oil, eggs and sour cream together until well mixed. Pour batter into a greased 13"x9" baking pan; set aside. Mix together brown sugar and cinnamon. Sprinkle mixture over batter; swirl into batter with a table knife. Bake at 325 degrees for 40 minutes. Whisk together remaining ingredients; pour over cake while still warm.

Most muffin batters can be stirred up the night before,
and can even be scooped into muffin cups. Simply cover and
refrigerate...in the morning, pop them in the oven. Your family
will love waking up to the sweet smell of muffins baking!

Quick Poppy Seed Muffins

Makes 2 dozen

18-1/4 oz. pkg. lemon cake mix
   with pudding

1/2 c. poppy seed
Garnish: sugar

Prepare cake mix according to package directions. Stir in poppy seed. Fill greased muffin cups 2/3 full. Top each muffin with a sprinkle of sugar. Bake at 350 degrees for about 8 to 10 minutes, until muffins test done.

Whip up a crock of honey butter to serve with warm cornbread.
Simply blend one cup honey with one cup softened butter
and one teaspoon vanilla extract.

Easy Cornbread

Makes 10 to 12 servings

8-1/2 oz. pkg. corn muffin mix   1/3 c. milk
8-1/2 oz. pkg. yellow cake mix   1/2 c. water
2 eggs, beaten

Combine all ingredients; mix well. Spread batter in a greased
13"x9" baking pan. Bake at 350 degrees for 15 to 20 minutes. Cut
into squares.

Serve breakfast juices in glasses with a bit of sparkle. Run a
lemon wedge around the rims of glasses, then dip rims in
superfine sugar. Garnish each with a sprig of fresh mint.

Graham-Streusel Coffee Cake

Serves 12 to 16

1-1/2 c. graham crackers, crushed
3/4 c. chopped walnuts
3/4 c. brown sugar, packed
1-1/2 t. cinnamon
2/3 c. margarine, melted

18-1/2 oz. pkg. yellow cake mix
1 c. water
1/4 c. oil
3 eggs

Combine cracker crumbs, walnuts, brown sugar and cinnamon; stir in margarine. Set aside. In a separate bowl, combine dry cake mix, water, oil and eggs; beat with an electric mixer on medium speed for 1-1/2 minutes. Pour half of batter into a greased 13"x9" baking pan; sprinkle with half the crumb mixture. Spoon remaining cake batter over the top; sprinkle with remaining crumb mixture. Bake at 350 degrees for 35 to 40 minutes; cool. Drizzle Powdered Sugar Icing over the top.

Powdered Sugar Icing:
1 c. powdered sugar
1 t. vanilla extract

2 to 4 T. water

Mix sugar, vanilla and enough water to make a drizzling consistency.

A baker's secret! Grease muffin cups on the bottoms
and just halfway up the sides...muffins will bake up
nicely puffed on top.

Yummy Carrot-Raisin Muffins

Makes one dozen

18-oz. pkg. carrot cake mix
15-oz. can pumpkin

1/3 c. golden raisins

Mix dry cake mix and pumpkin together to make a very thick batter. Add raisins and mix well. Fill paper-lined muffin cups 2/3 full. Bake at 400 degrees for 20 minutes, until muffins test done.

Make treats ahead of time and keep them frozen for
last-minute gifts. Freeze pies up to four months, breads
up to three months, cheesecakes up to 30 days and baked,
unfrosted cookies up to six months. Be sure they
are airtight, labeled and dated.

Busy-Morning Banana Bread

Makes 2 loaves

3 ripe bananas, mashed
3 eggs, beaten
1/2 c. butter, melted

1 T. vanilla extract
1/2 c. water
18-1/2 oz. pkg. yellow cake mix

In a large bowl, blend together bananas, eggs, butter, vanilla and water. Gradually add dry cake mix; beat for 4 minutes with an electric mixer on medium speed. Pour batter into 2 greased 9"x5" loaf pans. Bake at 350 degrees for 40 minutes. Increase temperature to 400 degrees and bake an additional 5 to 10 minutes, until tops are golden.

Add some chocolate chips to a favorite muffin recipe
for an extra sprinkle of sweetness.

So-Easy Pumpkin Muffins

Makes one dozen

18-1/4 oz. pkg. spice cake mix   1 c. water
15-oz. can pumpkin

In a bowl, blend dry cake mix and remaining ingredients together until well mixed. Fill lightly greased muffin cups 2/3 full. Bake at 350 degrees for 20 minutes, or until a toothpick inserted into center comes out clean.

A jar of honey is a sweet addition to the breakfast table
to enjoy on hot biscuits, toast or pancakes...even drizzled in
a steamy cup of hot tea. Pick up flavors like orange blossom
and wildflower at a farmers' market. Be sure to add
a wooden honey dipper too!

Simple Crumb Cake

Makes 12 to 16 servings

18-1/2 oz. pkg. yellow or white
    cake mix
2/3 c. milk

2/3 c. oil
4 eggs, beaten
Garnish: powdered sugar

Mix together dry cake mix, milk, oil and eggs. Spread batter in a greased 13"x9" baking pan. Bake at 350 degrees for 15 minutes. Let cool. Spread Crumb Topping over cake. Bake an additional 15 to 20 minutes. Cool. Sift powdered sugar on top.

Crumb Topping:

3 c. all-purpose flour
1/2 c. powdered sugar
1/2 c. brown sugar, packed

2 T. cinnamon
1/2 c. butter, melted
1 T. vanilla extract

Mix together flour, sugars and cinnamon. Mix butter and vanilla; pour into flour mixture. Stir until crumbly.

Thread cranberries and grapes onto wooden skewers
and serve with any breakfast beverage...looks pretty
in orange juice or white grape juice.

Citrus Coffee Cake

Serves 12 to 15

18-1/4 oz. pkg. white cake mix
1/2 c. warm water
1 env. active dry yeast
2 eggs, beaten
1/4 c. orange juice

1/2 c. all-purpose flour
1 c. brown sugar, packed
1 T. cinnamon
1/4 c. margarine, softened

In a large bowl, combine dry cake mix, water, yeast, eggs and orange juice; pour half the batter into a greased and floured Bundt® pan. Set aside. Combine remaining ingredients; sprinkle over batter in pan. Top with remaining batter; bake at 350 degrees for 30 to 40 minutes until center tests done. Invert onto a serving plate; drizzle Glaze over warm cake.

Glaze:

1 c. powdered sugar
2 T. margarine, softened

2 to 3 T. orange juice

Gently mix ingredients together until smooth and creamy; add additional orange juice to reach desired drizzling consistency.

A fragrant cup of cinnamon coffee is the perfect partner for fresh-baked treats. Just add a teaspoon of cinnamon and 1/4 cup of brown sugar to the coffeepot before brewing.

Brown Sugar Breakfast Rolls

Makes 16

3 envs. active dry yeast
2-1/2 c. warm water
18-1/4 oz. pkg. white cake mix
4-1/2 c. all-purpose flour, divided
1/2 c. butter, softened

1/2 c. brown sugar, packed
2 t. cinnamon
1/4 c. butter, melted
1/3 c. sugar

Dissolve yeast in warm water in a small bowl; set aside until creamy, about 10 minutes. Combine dry cake mix, 3 cups flour and yeast mixture; stir well. Mix in remaining flour 1/2 cup at a time; knead until smooth, about 8 minutes. Place in a greased bowl, turning to coat both sides; cover with a damp tea towel and set aside until double in bulk. Punch dough down; roll out on a lightly floured surface into a 16"x10" rectangle. Spread with softened butter; sprinkle with brown sugar and cinnamon. Roll up jelly-roll style beginning with a long edge; cut into one-inch slices. Whisk melted butter and sugar together; dip top of each roll into sugar mixture. Arrange in a greased 13"x9" baking pan; cover and let rise until double in bulk. Bake at 350 degrees until golden, about 20 minutes.

INDEX

INDEX

Our Story

Back in 1984, we were next-door neighbors raising our families in the little town of Delaware, Ohio. Two moms with small children, we were looking for a way to do what we loved and stay home with the kids too. We had always shared a love of home cooking and making memories with family & friends and so, after many a conversation over the backyard fence, **Gooseberry Patch** was born.

We put together our first catalog at our kitchen tables, enlisting the help of our loved ones wherever we could. From that very first mailing, we found an immediate connection with many of our customers and it wasn't long before we began receiving letters, photos and recipes from these new friends. In 1992, we put together our very first cookbook, compiled from hundreds of these recipes and, the rest, as they say, is history.

Hard to believe it's been over 25 years since those kitchen-table days! From that original little **Gooseberry Patch** family, we've grown to include an amazing group of creative folks who love cooking, decorating and creating as much as we do. Today, we're best known for our homestyle, family-friendly cookbooks, now recognized as national bestsellers.

One thing's for sure, we couldn't have done it without our friends all across the country. Each year, we're honored to turn thousands of your recipes into our collectible cookbooks. Our hope is that each book captures the stories and heart of all of you who have shared with us. Whether you've been with us since the beginning or are just discovering us, welcome to the **Gooseberry Patch** family!

Jo Ann & Vickie

Visit our website anytime
www.gooseberrypatch.com

Join Our Circle of Friends

You Tube

Read Our Blog

Find us on Facebook

Follow us on twitter

Pinterest

1·800·854·6673